I0504808

TAKE CONTROL OF YOUR MONEY........

INVEST

SUCCESSFULLY

IN WALL STREET

BY: AN INVESTMENT ADVISOR/M.D.

CONTENT	**PAGE NUMBER**

THIS BOOK IS DEDICATED TO

ALL THE GOOD

PEOPLE IN THIS

WORLD

Copyright c 2020 by Lotus 2014 LLC. All rights reserved. Created in the United States of America. Except as permitted under the United States Copyright Act of 1976, no part of this publication may be reproduced or distributed in any form or by any means, or stored in a data base or retrieval system, without prior written permission of the publisher.

Filed on 3/1/2020

Registration Number : pending

Title of Work: TAKE CONTROL OF YOUR MONEY........INVEST SUCCESSFULLY IN WALL STREET

Year of Completion: 2020

Author: An Investment Advisor/M.D.

Certification Date: pending

DISCLAIMER

This book is intended for educational purposes only. Investing in securities like stocks, mutual funds, options, futures, commodities and others carry significant risk. If you need professional investment advice you should consult a registered investment advisor and a financial planner. This book contains the author's opinions. The author does not have any financial interest in any of the business entities or companies mentioned in this book. The author may own some of the securities mentioned in this book. This book is sold with the understanding that neither the author nor the publisher is engaged in rendering financial, legal, accounting or other professional services. If you need any of these services, you should seek the advice of a professional person. You should consider virtual/paper trading before investing your hard-earned money. You should consider the possible risks of investing in the stock market and consider your investment goals and risk tolerance before investing. You should understand that past performance does not guarantee future results. By reading this book you are implicitly agreeing to these terms.

FOREWORD

I have a question for you. Do you want to make money in the stock market or own stocks? This book is aimed at helping the former. The ancient method of buying and holding does not work anymore in the present-day stock market except for retirement accounts and children's educational accounts where you invest in exchange traded funds. Millions of dollars are invested only for a few seconds and trading is done by super computers.

First of all, I want to tell you that there is lot of money to be made in the stock market. According to Barron's the U.S.stock market was worth $33 trillion in January of 2018. This calculation was made on the total market capitalization of the Russell 3000 index which covers 98.5% of the market capitalization of all the U.S. stocks. This was around $18 trillion in 2014. Out of this around $4 trillion is invested in over 5000 exchange traded funds as of 2019. In 2014 it was around $2 trillion. Later I will discuss about exchange traded funds or ETFs.

The richest people in the world invest in the U.S. stock market with only one goal, to make money. Yes. You can make lot of money consistently if you follow a method. If you do not, you will be thrown into the arena with lions. Listen, you are competing with professionals who are investing big money, using fast computers and thus controlling the market. Investments from individuals constitute only about 15%. Individual investors like you and me do not control the market. We are followers. From 1997 through 2016 individual investors earned about 3.98% annually whereas the S&P index went up by 10.6% annually. If you do not have a formula, you can become a millionaire very quickly, if you started as a billionaire!!

I have listed a number of formulas to choose from. You can use one or more depending on your liking and style. You need discipline. If you waver you lose. Like in baseball, you hit and run. That is the way to make money by trading. You will see opportunities. Do not fail to take them. You cannot buy stocks whenever you want and hope that they would go up. You cannot cheer them and make them go up. Market trend is one of the most important factors. Trend is not only your friend but also your lifeline. Do not fight the trend. At times you have to be out of the market completely to protect your assets.

Wait patiently. Bear markets do not last forever. Cash is king during these periods. The market does not care whether you make money or not; nor about your finances. You take charge and be the pilot. The market is alive and has its own mind and behavior. It is not rational all the time which creates opportunities for you and me.

Goal

Create profits

Realize profits

Enjoy the fruits of profits

Give to charity

When you have 20% profits take that amount out of the equities. You may keep it as cash or pay part of your home mortgage or car loan, etc. If you do not take profits, they will vanish. If you raise cash, you can use it later when the market is down and stocks are on "sale". If you are fully invested all the time and the market goes down, you will not have funds to buy your favorite stocks at a discount. The market can go down suddenly for no reason or following some adverse event. I met a gentleman who showed me his Porsche Carrera which he bought from the profits he made in the stock market. He was buying and selling only one stock, Cisco from 1995 to 1999. Every few days he would buy and sell. He was adding the profits to his principal. The stock went up from around $2.5 to around $50 (prices adjusted for splits). He smartly cashed out in 1999.

GOLDEN WORDS OF WISDOM

Do not believe in anything simply because you have heard it. Do not believe in anything simply because it is spoken and rumored by many. Do not believe in anything simply because it is found written in books. Do not believe in anything merely on the authority of your elders. Do not believe in traditions because they have been handed down for many generations. But after OBSERVATION and ANALYSIS, when you find that anything AGREES WITH REASON, then accept it and live up to it.

(Would you believe that these words were uttered around 2500 years ago by Gautama Buddha and they apply so well to the stock market today?)

SEVEN PEARLS FOR SUCCESS

Success in investing is similar to stringing a pearl necklace. Any missing pearl can ruin the necklace.

You need the following 7 pearls:

1. Understanding yourself
2. Understanding the market
3. Right information
4. Right tools
5. Common sense
6. Sticking to rules rigidly
7. Nerves of steel

If you have the discipline and strong will power to follow these seven rules you can make tremendous profits and making the journey safe and enjoyable. Focus on blocking unnecessary noise, setting financial goals, learning from the Masters, learning from past mistakes and not repeating them, not following newsletters that are based on probabilities; do not try to forecast the future. Do create portfolios that run on autopilot, detaching emotionally from the market, picking up great value stocks after a market crash, understanding that the risk is not in our securities but in ourselves, having proper judgment, having the courage to take advantage of opportunities that knock on our doors and avoiding overpriced securities due to emotional attachment. Do constantly look for beaten down stocks of great companies, having the courage to buy when everybody is scared and having the courage to sell when everybody is frantically buying.

HOW DO YOU FIND A GOOD BROKER?

First of all, you have to open an account in a good brokerage firm with good reputation, high ranking for good execution of your orders and inexpensive. Also, the company should have a solid balance sheet of their own. The company should be rock solid so that it would be in existence when you retire.

What happens when your stockbroker goes bankrupt? The Securities Investor Protection Corporation (SIPC) protects client's cash and securities such as stocks and bonds. However, commodity contracts, limited partnerships, and the fixed annuities are not protected. There is also a limit per customer account. SIPC the covered up to $500,000 of which $250,000 may be in cash. You should make sure that your broker is a member of SIPC. Many brokerage firms have their own supplemental insurance in addition.

Please read the following: https://www.finra.org/investors/alerts/if-brokerage-firm-closes-its-doors

If your brokerage firm goes bankrupt, you have to file a claim before the deadline. There is a trustee who has been appointed who will evaluate your claim. You will get paid when the liquidation process starts. Some of your assets may be missing. Also, there could be considerable delay in getting your funds. So, what do you do? Before you open an account in a brokerage firm get that balance sheet. This will show you whether this broker has too much debt and can go bankrupt. You can also go to Finance.Yahoo.com and check the balance sheet of the brokerage firm your considering if their company is listed. For e.g. as of 2/25/2020 Charles Schwab has a total debt/equity ratio of 44.78. This is quite good. So, you evaluate your brokerage company this way and choose a broker that is least likely to go bankrupt.

You can go to Google.com and search for a good broker. In the olden days it used to cost a lot of money to make a trade. Now most brokerage firms do not charge for buying or selling stocks or ETFs. So, this is an additional saving for you. Some of them do not charge for even option trades.

In addition to a commission free account, you open an account in TD Ameritrade because it has the best software platform, which is free, called Thinkorswim. Many brilliant traders have contributed a number of technical trading methods in this platform which you can use and make good money. Kiplinger's gave an award in 2018 as #1 overall broker. TD Ameritrade has been acquired by Charles Schwab Corporation. You will read more on the applications of Thinkorswim later in this book.

Summary:

- Select a high-ranking broker with low total debt/equity
- Please read the following:
  https://www.finra.org/investors/alerts/if-brokerage-firm-closes-its-doors

BUYING

HOW DO I SELECT MY STOCKS?

I want to invest in the very best stocks. I go to Investors Business Daily, section D. it lists 7000 stocks in alphabetical order. In the second column earnings-per-share growth rating is given for each stock. I select the ones which have the highest rating, consisting of 99, 98, 97, 96 AND 95. There are usually around 260 stocks. I create a watchlist in Vectorvest (which is a subscription-based software program) and import these stocks. Vectorvest gives me many details about these stocks like price, value, growth rate, sales growth rate, earnings yield (inverse of price/earnings ratio), price-earnings ratio, dividend yield etc. Value is calculated from forecasted earnings per share, forecasted earnings growth, profit, interest rate and inflation rate. Thus, I can rank them using any of the above factors. I have created a column for value/price. I look at these stocks in the descending order of value/price. I select 10 stocks with highest ratio of value over price. I select stocks from different sectors. This reduces risk. I avoid stocks which have less than $1 billion in market capitalization. I also avoid stocks which have an average daily volume of less than 100,000. This makes it easier to sell and also the spread between the bid and ask prices would be less. I avoid stocks priced less than $15 as they are more volatile. Most mutual funds invest in stocks priced over $15. I eliminate any stock which has a debt of more than 40%. I like stocks which have a return on equity (ROE) of more than 20%, sales of more than 20%, earnings growth of more than 20%.

I go to Finance.Yahoo.com to study the profile, key statistics, cash flow and balance sheet. I look at the book value of the stock also. I look at the cash flow to see whether it is positive and that it is increasing every year. In the balance sheet I look at the total current assets and the total liabilities. If the total current assets are more than the total liabilities of a company, it's a great situation. This means that the company can pay off all their debt anytime. I also go to www.SEC.gov and read the most recent annual report of the company.

Occasionally there are special situations. Green Mountain coffee (GMCR) was selling at the $110 on 9/21/2011. It was a top-rated company in Investors Business Daily. It fell to a price of $17 on 7/23/2012 due to some rumors. The fundamentals were still excellent and it was a great opportunity to buy on 7/23/2012. By 11/17/ 2014 the price had gone up to $155. Similarly, you will be able to pick up some gems at throwaway prices if you look at the stocks that have been beaten down. That is why you have to keep good amount of cash all the time. Opportunities knock on your door frequently. Beaten down value stocks may take even a year to go to the top. The profit on such transactions will be huge but patience is needed. I also choose stocks from this group which have momentum and relative strength. These stocks will appreciate fast.

Once I buy, let's say, 10 stocks, then I watch them closely in my Thinkorswim software (of TD Ameritrade). In Thinkorswim software, I use TTM scalper alert, one-year daily chart. This gives me buy signal with arrow pointing up and sell signal with arrow pointing down. This indicator has been developed by master trader John Carter. His observation is that most trend reversals occur after three consecutive higher or lower closes. This indicator shows me the change in the trend. Learn how to use this method by watching videos in Youtube; also, by reading John F. Carter's book named Mastering the Trade. This is the primary indicator I use for any stock or ETF and it has worked very well for me. In the chart mode, I have added RSI which also helps in judging the direction of the stock or ETF and whether it is oversold or overbought. I have included on balance volume which tells me about accumulation/distribution of the stock or ETF. I also have added TTM squeeze (by John Carter also) which gives me a histogram and the direction of the stock or ETF. Momentum is very helpful. If the momentum is on the way down and crosses the 0 line to the downside, it is better to sell. It is good to check the weekly chart of the stock to see in which direction it is going, before you buy. I have MACD in my charts also. All these above indicators help me buy and sell stocks, ETFs or options, rationally and profitably.

Summary:

- Investors Business Daily – Section D – Select stocks with EPS rating of 95-99.
- Select stocks out of this list based on fundamentals.
- Take the opportunity when some of these stocks are beaten down.
- Buy about 10 stocks and monitor closely. Sell if they go down by 10%.
- Invest gradually into each stock by splitting your money in 3 parts.

BUYING STOCKS FOR THE LONG TERM

You always keep a list of stocks that you would like to own. Have good amount of cash. When the stock you like has dropped by 50% or 60% jump in and buy. This is the time when there is blood on Wall Street. You invest in the best companies which will be alive and well decades from now. Buy only when these stocks have good value. You can use Vectorvest to get this information or go to Finance.Yahoo.com and calculate yourself. You presume that you are buying this company and analyze the revenue, income, cash flow, balance sheet, etc. This is how Warren Buffett would buy. He waits a year or many years to buy the right stock at the right time. You can always buy for 1/3 of the money you were going to invest in that stock and then invest the next 1/3 after the stock goes up, as the uptrend becomes clear. You can invest the last third after the equity goes up a little more. Then wait patiently for the equity to go back up to its intrinsic value. This may take a year or more. If you sell at that time your equity should have gone up by 50% or 60. Warren Buffett buys equities at the right time and keeps them for many years so that the compounding of earnings growth will make the investment extremely valuable. Warren Buffett's portfolio had produced an average annual compounding rate of return of 23.8% in 32 years ending in 1998 as noted in the book called Buffettology written by his daughter in law Mary Buffet and David Clark.

"Warren believes that compounding is the secret to getting really rich", Buffettolgy by Mary Buffett & David Clark.

The following is another quotation from the same book. "If your investments grow at 15% to 25% a year, if you started with $1 million, in 30 years, you will have, max, $807 million... What? No. 807 billion dollars!!!"

The rich Medici family in Italy Invested funds equal to $100,000, six hundred years ago. The funds grew at 5% annually. It grew to five hundred and seventeen quadrillion ($517,100,000,000,000,000). Reported by Frank A. Vanderlip in 1933. Amazing!!

What you need is time on your side for your investment to grow. The investment should be good, stable and powerful and has proven by making good profits year over year (compounded growth). In this book you will find your answer and the secret to success. You do not need any other outside help. You trust in yourself and in this book and follow the guidelines to success.

Lot of people lose money by trading in the stock market because they do not have a method. There is too much information out there. You need the right information to make money.

BUY TWO SHARES IN SEVERAL GREAT ONES FOR THE LONG TERM: Nowadays most brokerage firms do not charge any fees for transacting stocks or ETFs. So, when a great new IPO comes out or when a great stock is selling at deep discount, you may buy two shares of such company. When the stock price doubles sell one and keep the other for many years. Tesla went public around July of 2010 around $20. On 2/19/2020 it closed at $917, 4585% appreciation in 10 years!

SUMMARY

- You can make millions in Wall Street if you rigidly follow a method.
- Compounding is the secret to getting filthy rich.
- You need at least fifteen years to achieve a huge amount for your retirement.
- You should use a tax deferred account in a solid brokerage company.

TRADING STOCKS

You should choose very strong companies that have monopoly in their fields and have a moat around them. These should be large capitalized stocks with low debt and have shown good growth rates in sales and earnings year over year. On 2/25/2020 in Vectorvest I screened all the stocks which have over $10 billion in market capitalization. I had a total of 974 stocks. Then I used the following filters: sales growth of 15% a year, earnings growth of 15% a year and safety rank of 1 or more in Vectorvest. I ran a back test. The growth in the following stocks from 2/25/2015 to 2/25/2020: NFLX 427%, CRM 188%, NEE 160%, AMT 152%, AVGO 151%, SBAC 143%, TMO 136% and AAPL 124%. During the same time S&P went up by 48%. So surely you are picking up gems this way. These companies are strong with excellent sales and earnings growth.

Look at the chart of VIX every day. VIX is the volatility index for S&P 500. It's also the fear index. When the stock market starts going down VIX starts going up. In minor stock market connections VIX made go up to 20. On 10/24 /2008 VIX went up over 79 and the market had crashed at that time. This would be a good time to start investing in stocks gradually.

Every 2 months or so the market goes down a bit, may be by 5%. Every six months or so it is down more, may be 10% or even more; this happens usually in October and March. In October fund managers sell their laggards and then reinvest that money in beaten down sectors. After the market corrects money again flows back in and stock prices start going up. So, there is a seasonal pattern.

If someone says that you cannot time the market, walk away. **YES. YOU CAN TIME THE MARKET BY FOLLOWING THE TREND.** When the trend is up you go long and when the trend is broken you go to cash. I am subscriber to Vectorvest, Inc. Their signals are great, especially the sell signals. Of course, with any trend following system, you may get whipsawed.

You cannot avoid it. You can get in again when there is a buy signal. THIS EXERCISE WILL PREVENT YOU FROM LOSING BIG MONEY. Because when the down trend starts the market can go down even more than 20%. Let us say that the S&P 500 goes down by 25%, your stock may go down by 50%. To break even again, your stock has to go up 100%! In volatile markets you can get whipsawed and trend following systems will not help.

If you are fully invested all the time in the market, when it crashes, you will lose money and you will not have money to invest. It is better to keep cash and invest when there are opportunities. Patience is needed. I always pray to God; God give me patience but give it to me now!.

You can use Stockcharts.com, for timing. It is a free website. You can look at the charts of VTSMX (Vanguard Total Stock Market Index Fund), DIA (Spider Dow Jones Industrials ETF), SPY (Spider S&P 500 ETF), QQQ (NASDAQ 100 ETF) and IWM (Russell 200 Small Cap Index ETF). You look at these graphs at the end of each day. Look at the MACD in the bottom which will tell you where you stand now and when to buy and when to sell. You can learn about MACD in their Chartschool. The best time to invest is when the black fast-moving line crosses from below to above the red slow-moving line. The opposite is true for selling. When the market goes sideways these lines can overlap and make it difficult to judge. Then you look at the price action of the chart and use the 50-day moving average. If your stock price goes below that, you should sell.

Later on, I will be talking about long term investment in detail, where you do not time the market. This is for children's accounts and your retirement accounts. In this scenario you invest a fixed amount of money every two weeks or four weeks on a regular basis irrespective of where the market is currently, into an ETF. You will be amazed by the wealth accumulated years later.

For trading purposes, you have to time the market; Buy when your favorite indicator or indicators give you a buy signal. Then based on your taste hold it using the day chart until you get a sell signal. Then sell that stock and go to cash. I do not advise day trading. If you do not follow charts and signals, you will lose money and sleep. You can get lot of stress which can affect your health and the family relationships.

Every evening you should look at your stocks and the list of charts like VTSMX, DIA, SPY, QQQ, IWM and VIX.

Here is a chart of Vanguard Index Trust Total Stock Market Index:

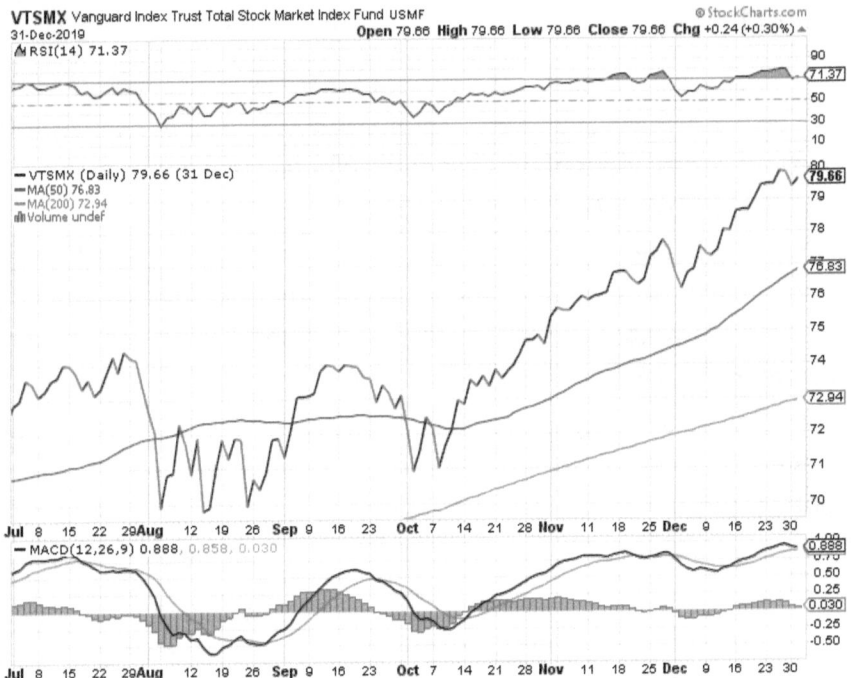

Stockcharts.com (free) has superb charts for any stock or ETF and there are moving averages given. In "Stockcharts.com" at the top you will find a blank space to the right of "SharpChart". You can enter the symbol for any stock or ETF. Below the graph you will find "Chart Attributes". I recommend that you look at Daily as well as Weekly charts. For weekly you choose a five-year period.

You can choose Candlesticks or solid thick line. The 50 day and 200 day moving averages are shown in the daily chart. RSI and MACD are given in the chart. You can study them and the direction of the market will be clear. Direction of the market is an important factor. Even if you own great stocks, most of them will go down during a downturn in the market.

Also, you should look at the graph of RSI (Relative Strength Index) which is above the chart. If the RSI hits 70 and stays there and starts moving down it shows a downtrend in the stock. If it hits 30 and starts going up the stock is in uptrend. Below the chart is MACD (Moving Average Convergence Divergence using 12,26, 9). When the fast-moving line goes above the slow-moving line, uptrend is starting and vice versa. Please study the daily and weekly charts. Once you buy a stock use these charts and technical indicators to get in and out.

Pay attention to seasonality in the stock market. In the next few pages you will find Seasonality Charts of SPY (an ETF investing in S & P 500), DIA (an ETF investing in Dow Jones Industrial Average), QQQ (an ETF investing in the 100 largest capitalized stocks in NASDAQ) and IWM (an ETF investing in Russell 2000). You can go to StockCharts.com (free charting service). In top center you will see "sharp chart". You scroll down to "seasonality". Then to the right enter "QQQ" for example. You can make more money with this knowledge. If you invest/trade in these four ETFs you can make a lot of money without depending on individual stocks where the risk and reward are higher.

FOR ANY STOCK, ETF OR OPTION USE TDAMERITRADE'S THINKORSWIM SOFTWARE FOR TRADING

This is my favorite method. You have to have an account in TD Ameritrade. Then you can download the free software platform called Thinkorswim. It is the best software I have ever used. Many great traders and famous investors have contributed their own methods. There are numerous ones available. The major ones I use are developed by Mr. John Carter. He is the founder of SimplerTrading.com. He frequently appears on TV business channels, money shows, Traders' Expos, etc. His Mastering the Trade is in its 3rd edition.

If you have any problems setting up the following up call TD Ameritrade and they will guide you. First of all, go into your account and download Thinkorswim platform. Then go to "Studies" in the top right and click on it. You will have a scroll down window. In that select "Add study". Then select "All studies". Then scroll down to John Carter's studies. Then another window opens up and you select "TTM Scalper Alert". Then save this study set as "ABC or whatever name you give". Next hit edit studies. A large window opens to the left. I choose the following one at a time. 1. Bollinger Bands (I use the standard numbers). Then I hit "Add selected". It moves to the right. I move it up to the top. I bring the TTM Scalper Alert to the same area called "Price". 2. Keltner Channels (I use the standard numbers). I also bring it to the same area called "Price". 3. I select TTM Squeeze and move it to the right and move it to the box called "Volume". Then I bring in OnBalanceVolume and bring it to the box called "Volume". Then I bring in RSI and place it in the lower compartment. I click on the cogwheel to the right of it and change the RSI length to 4. You are all set now.

In the top where you selected "Studies", to the left of it is the Time frame. You can choose from the list given from 1 minute to 1 week. It depends on how you trade. I use one year/one day for fairly long-term investments. I choose 20 day/1-hour chart for trading short terms like a day or two. This set has made more money for me than anything else.

Savvy investors do not lose big money in the market. What they do is that as soon as they buy a stock, they note down that they would sell if the stock price goes 10% below the purchase price. They do not question when that loss is triggered, they sell. Let your winners run and cut the losers early.

Summary:

- Invest in strong companies which have monopoly in their fields.
- Market trend makes or breaks your account. Follow VIX daily; look at the chart of VTSMX, DIA, SPY, QQQ and IWM in Stockcharts.com daily. Look at MACD to see whether it is favorable or not.
- For trading any stock or ETF I find TDAmeritrade's Thinkorswim to be the best software and it is free for their clients.

SEVERAL QUESTIONS AND ANSWERS

When is the very best time to invest?

When there is a 'sale' in the market. On 10/23/2014 I received a sale booklet from Macy's. From 10/28/2014 for six days there would be a storewide sale and the prices would be 60% to 85% off. What a beautiful scenario! Let us apply the same philosophy for buying stocks. So why not buy stocks when they are on sale. Also, when you buy stocks near their book value or intrinsic value the chances are low that the price would go down significantly more. **THE ONLY CONTROL YOU HAVE IN THE STOCK MARKET IS THE PRICE YOU PAY FOR THE STOCKS.**

How many stocks should you own? In a personal portfolio ten stocks should be adequate. Invest in different industry groups so that you are diversified.

Should you borrow and buy stocks on margin?
Never. It's a risky and lot of people lose lots of money because of this.

What is the market price of a stock based on?
The most important factor is demand/supply; mass psychology; the fundamentals of the stock.

Is buy and hold a good method of investing?
It is the only way to invest for the long term. As I mentioned before it is great for children's accounts like Coverdell education savings account (ESA) and 529 college fund. These two have tax advantages. Other major long-term investments are 401 K, other pension plan trusts, etc. After years due the beauty of compounding the results would be Himalayan.

If your goal is not long term, then buy and hold will lead to disaster. Every stock goes up and down. This is because mutual funds, hedge funds, and institutions invest in different sectors at different times. Every quarter they adjust their portfolios. They sell their stocks in which they have gains and invest in beaten down sectors.

Also, there are professionals who short stocks all the time. They sell first and then when the price of the stock goes down, they buy back.

So, the very best time to invest is to wait for the opportune time. Buy when stocks are on "sale". Then follow charts using technical analysis, for e.g. MACD, RS, TTM scalper alert, TTM squeeze, etc. and sell and go to cash. You can use that money to buy another stock selling below its intrinsic value and technical analysis shows that it has bottomed and is in an uptrend now. Keep on using your money to the maximum benefit by rotating into different opportunities to make your money grow fast. Short runs are better than holding a stock long-term. Short-term trading is a better business. Don't be married to any stock. Choose fast moving stocks than the slow ones. Stock market can suddenly turn for no reason or some reason. When the institutional investors run for the exits the market goes down in a fast and furious way. Also, there are super computers which are programmed to buy and sell huge number of stocks and ETFs. When the market goes up it crawls up.

Below is a picture of the Joplin tornado of 2011. When the market corrects your brokerage account can look like this. It takes a long time to repair the damage.

Curtesy of Wikipedia.org

Formed	May 22, 2011, 5:34 p.m. CDT(UTC–05:00)
Duration	38 minutes
Dissipated	May 22, 2011, 6:12 p.m. CDT (UTC–05:00)
Maxrating[1]	EF5 tornado
Highest winds	•> 200 mph (320 km/h)
Damage	$2.8 billion (2011 USD) (Costliest tornado in U.S. history) $3.12 billion (2019 USD[1])
Fatalities	158 direct fatalities (+3 indirect), 1,150 injuries[2][3][4]

What are some of the information which can tell you when the stock market is too overvalued or undervalued?

1. Period please check out the following website for valuable information :

https://money.cnn.com/data/fear-and-greed/

2. A great one is Shiller PE, developed by Prof. Robert Shiller of Yale University. It is calculated using the following formula:

1. Use the annual earnings of the S&P 500 companies over the past 10 years.
2. Adjust the past earnings for inflation using CPI; past earnings are adjusted to today's dollars.
3. Average the adjusted values for E10.
4. The Shiller P/E equals the ratio of the price of the S&P 500 index over E10.
   Historical low: 4.8
   Historical high: 44.2

If the Shiller is PE is higher than the historical mean of 17, your investments in future will be low. It is better to invest less money and watch closely in this scenario. If it below 17 your investments will make more money.

How do you trade safely?

You have to detach from the crowd. If the market is overvalued and the crowd is in a frenzy to buy you sell your stocks, raise cash and keep quiet. If the market crashes, if there is blood on the street, you step in and buy your favorite stocks at fire sale prices. Then wait patiently until your stocks reach their intrinsic value.

What is the most important factor in evaluating a stock for a buy?

Price movement reflects everything. Is the stock going up and has a high demand/supply? The next most important item is volume. Is the stock price going up with higher than usual volume? This would be a good scenario.

If a stock declines over a long period of time and suddenly shows a large volume with the stock turning up, it is extremely bullish. Buy the best stocks when they are beaten down due to sector rotation or in a market crash. Look at the value/price ratio. If you buy an overpriced stock and it corrects quickly it may take a long time to recover or it may not recover. You have to buy the best stock, meaning a great company, with capitalization over $10 billion, sales growth rate going up every year for the past 3 years over 15% each year, earnings growth going up every year for the past 3 years over 15% each year and a safe growth company.

What are the characteristics of a company whose shares would appreciate a lot?

Old established companies may be growing at only 10% a year. Do not invest in these. Look for companies that have come into the market within the past 15 years and have been growing rapidly. Their sales should be going at 15% or more a year. Their earnings should be going up at 15% or more a year, more the better. Choose companies which have less than 40% debt/equity. Look for companies which have no competition in that arena. Invest in companies which have return on equity of more than 20%, more the better. Go to finance.yahoo.com. You can get all the above information. In the balance sheet look at the current assets. In the current assets are more than the total liabilities, it's a great situation.

This company can pay off its debt anytime. Companies with new products and new technology will appreciate a lot. Companies with new leadership, like new CEOs will do well. When you look at the earnings of a company, look for significant growth in the last few quarters and in the last few years. A great management is an asset.

How do you find bargain stocks?
Keep looking at stocks hitting 52-week lows. NASDAQ.COM lists NASDAQ 52-week low stocks. You have a list of stocks and any stock from that list hits 52 week low, start watching it. Once it completes its downward journey and turns around and starts going up you can buy. Always you can invest 1/3 of what you want to invest in that stock and then when it goes up by 5%, invest the next 1/3 and then after it goes up another 1/3, invest the last third. MSN.com has a stock screener which gives stocks hitting new 52-week lows. Vectorvest has a research tool and it can show these also.

What about high priced stocks vs low priced stocks?
Avoid stocks selling for less than $15. Except for small cap funds, all other mutual funds invest in stocks which are priced $15 or more. The lower priced stocks are traded a lot and are very volatile. They may have high spread between the bid (the price you pay when you sell) and the ask (the price you pay when you buy). Also, if the average daily volume is less than 100,000 it may be hard for you to sell.

Is there an ideal or safe investment?
No. There is none. When the market is in downtrend cash is king. **Market trend is the most important factor in determining the value of your assets.** Trend is not only your friend but your life line. Stock market can go down without a warning at any time to any depth. The margin of safety lies in buying the very best stock at a bargain price.

Should you be invested in the market all the time?

Yes, only if your investments are for children or for retirement. Otherwise no. Trend is your friend and your lifeline. If you go against the trend you will lose. Keep lot of cash and be idle for long periods of time. Opportunities knock on your door. Do not miss those. Devote some time looking at the market and your portfolio every evening. Do not sell a position unless the technical indicators are violated. Your goal is to attain maximum profit and make the capital grow.

Sit on cash until you think that there is a very great chance that the stock under your consideration would go up. Invest in the best of the best. "Have the purchase price be so attractive that even a mediocre sale gives good results." (Warren Buffett). "The entrance strategy is actually more important than the exit strategy" (Eddie Lampert).

Should you place market orders or limit orders?

Never place a market order which means that the broker can give you any price. Always place a limit order and then change it as needed.

What is position sizing?

If you have $10,000 and they want to buy 10 different stocks you invest $1000 in each stock. This is called position sizing. You do this initially when you invest. As the market keeps going up and the trend is up, consider selling the laggards and pyramiding into the winning stocks. So, you may end up having much less than 10 stocks as the market keeps going up. At some point using the sell rules, sell everything and go to cash and wait for an opportunistic time.

Should you average down?

Only in children's accounts for education and in your retirement plans. Otherwise never. Adding to your position when your stock goes down is called averaging down. Do not do that. It leads to disaster. When your stock goes down by 10%, sell and don't ask questions. Lots of people lose lots of money averaging down. Luck and hope don't work. You cannot cheer your stock and make it go up.

Should you invest in dividend paying stocks?
No. Do not invest in stocks just to receive dividends. You may dividend payment but the stock may go down 10% in value and lost money. It is better to buy and sell stocks and make profit. I growth stocks looking for appreciation of your capital.

Should you get advice from a stockbroker?
Never. The broker will try to sell you stocks that are being promote his company. You be your own boss. You learn to invest by reading bo written by Masters in Wall Street.

Should you follow an analysts' opinions?
Never. They are always guessing and most of them are wrong, most of the time

Where do I park my cash?
On a short-term basis you may invest in T-bills or money market funds backed by U.S. government securities.

What about short selling?
Short selling involves selling a stock you do not own. The broker borrows it from somebody else and then sells it in your account. At some point you have to buy it back and return it. If the stock goes down you make money and if it goes up you lose money. You may consider subscribing SHORTSQUEEZE.COM. Without information noted in this website or a similar one it is difficult to practice short selling. If you become an expert in short selling your make good money. You can also buy contra ETFs which go up in value when the market goes down. For example, non-leveraged regular ETF for S&P 500 is SPY. The non-leveraged contra ETF for S&P 500 is SH. So, if the market is going down you can buy SH. There are also leveraged ETFs (for up or down) which move 2 to 3 times when compared to the non-leveraged ones. You can make more money quickly, if you time it properly.

OPTIONS

What are options?

You should learn how to use options. You will make more money and risk less. The Chicago Board of Options Exchange (CBOE) is the largest US options exchange in the world. In April 2019 from the first through the 28th, equity options traded were around 312 million and the index options where around 32 million. Options trading volume has been going up steadily for the past several years. A good options investor can make 500% or even 1000% on his investment in a few days. I want to give you an example. To buy 100 shares of Invesco QQQ ETF, you have to spend $19,062. This is as of 4/26/2019, at the close. Instead if you buy one contract of call with a strike price of $191, expiring on July 19, 2019, it would cost you $565 which is the ask price. There will be a commission added to this. So, by paying $565 your controlling 100 shares of QQQ until July 19, 2019. If QQQ goes up to $200 by July 19, 2019, the call contract gives you the right to buy 100 shares of QQQ at $191. Your profit is $900 minus $565 which you paid to buy this contract. Instead of buying you can close your contact at any time before its expiration on July 19, 2019.

This way you keep the gain minus the money you pay for, without buying the ETF. If QQQ keeps going down after you bought this contract, and on July 19, 2019 if the price of QQQ is less than $191, you will lose your investment of $565. If QQQ keeps going down, you can close the contract at any time before July 19, 2019, and take a partial loss. So, you buy a call option when you think that the stock or ETF is going up. The profits are unlimited and the risk is what you paid for your contract called the premium. When you buy a call option you are not obligated to buy the stock or ETF. When you buy a call or put option choose an expiration date at least 90 days away. This is because during the last 30 days, the option time premium will decay rapidly to 0 on the date of expiration. This is called theta.

When the option price is $191, if you choose a strike price of your call option at one $190, it is called in the money. So, there is one-dollar intrinsic value. If the strike price you chose is $191, it is at the money. If the strike price is $192 it's called out of the money. If you buy a call option in the money, for example, $181, then went QQQ goes up the option will gain almost as much as the gain in the ETF, on a daily basis. This is called Delta. Delta measures the change in the price of a stock option relative to the change in the price of the underlying stock.

A put option gives you the right to sell but not the obligation. If you think that the stock or ETF is going to go down you buy a put option. Once you do the above a couple of times you will gain the experience and confidence. The expiration date is always the third Friday of each month. Most options or monthly options. There are weekly of options available on some stocks and ETFs. There are also Long-Term Equity Anticipation Securities (LEAPS). These are options contracts with the expiration dates that are longer than one year.

Go to www.optionseducation.org. This site belongs to the Options Industry Council. You can learn a lot about options, the benefits and risks at this website. They offer superb educational programs.

How do you open an options account?
If you have no experience in options trading initially it may be difficult to open an options account. There are different levels of options trading. Try to get the approval to buy calls and puts. Instead of buying stocks and ETFs you can achieve the same by investing very small amounts in options. Talk to different brokers and try your very best to get approval for trading options. In the long run you would benefit a lot.

If you have $100,000 how much should you invest?
Here comes the importance of learning how to use options. I will give you an illustration. Let us say you want to buy 100 shares of QQQ as the trend is up. On 4/18/2019 it closed at $187. It would cost you $18,700. Let us presume that it would go up to $197 in one month. Your profit would be $1000 on an investment of $18,700.

Instead if you buy a call option on QQQ expiring on 7/19/2019 with the strike price of $187, it will cost you $629. So instead of risking $18,700 to control 100 shares, your risking $629 to control 100 shares for three months. If QQQ goes up to $197 in one month, you can close your position for a profit of $1000. If QQQ goes down below your strike price of $187 you will lose the entire premium of $629 on 7/19/2019. But you can close that position any day before 7/19/2019, which is the expiration date of the contract. If you are buying a call option and QQQ is trading at $ 187; if you choose a strike price below that, let us say $186 it is called "in the money". If the strike price you choose is $187 it is called "at the money"; and if the strike price is above $187 it is called "out of the money". As a general rule, in the money options will move more than the out of the money options. Short term options will move more than the longer-term options.

To me options are less risky and the gains are unlimited if you are buying a call or a put option. Start learning how to use calls and puts. Use them and gain experience. Later you can learn about all the other complex options strategies available to trade. When you buy a call or put it is called the opening transaction and when you get out it is called the closing transaction. Every option has a bid price and an ask price. When you do an opening transaction, you pay the ask price; when you close you get the bid price. Volatility is good for option traders who are in and out in a few days.

Should you sell covered call options?
No. If you buy a stock and sell a covered call option, if the stock goes up your stock will be taken away at the strike price. The stock may keep on going up after that and you lose the full benefit of getting into that stock. If the stock goes down a lot, the premium you got may not be significant.

What is married put?

If you buy a stock, you can buy a put option simultaneously which is called a married put. If the stock goes down the put option premium would go up. It works like insurance.

When do you sell put options?

You can sell put option on a stock that is in uptrend to create income. This is called a cash covered the put. The broker tells you how much cash you have to keep in the account to do this. As the stock price keeps going up the put premium will go down. On the expiration date if the stock price is higher than the option strike price, you keep all the premium. Most rich people sell put options to generate income. If the stock price goes down below the strike price, the stock will be assigned to you at the strike price. But you keep the premium. You can always close the option contract by buying it back before it expires.

When do you place a bull put spread?

If a stock is in uptrend, you can sell a put at a certain strike price. At the same time, you buy a put option with the same expiration date but with a lower strike price. This spread will limit your possible losses. But the gains are limited also. This method is less risky. You can always close either or both options at any time before the expiration date.

KNOWLEDGE AND SUCCESS

How do you make lots of money in the stock market?
Copy the masters. You have to learn to pyramid rather than diversify. G.M.Loeb, founding partner of E.F.Hutton always believed in "intelligent pyramiding". (You will read more about this later). You can start with very little capital and in a few decades you can become very rich. "I will tell you how to become rich. Close the doors. Be fearful when others are greedy. Be greedy when others are fearful". (Warren Buffettt). "We can do very well by only placing an occasional bet when the odds are heavily in our favor."" Few bets, big bets, infrequent bets" (The Dhandho investor, By Mohnish Pabrai). "That is one of the mysteries of our business and it is a mystery to me and to everybody else. But we know from experience that eventually the market catches up with value). (Benjamin Graham). **When you buy when the market is beaten down, you are basically buying a dollar bill for fifty cents or less.**

How does an investor succeed?
Success depends on your abilities and the setup you have. Overconfidence will kill you. If you are open minded and unbiased you will succeed. Use the sixth sense, common sense, which is not that common. Today there is information overload. **Information is not an effective substitute for thinking.** "Our life is frittered away by detail...simplify, simplify" (Henry Thoreau).

Do not forecast which way the market would go. Use charts. Learn to concentrate on the best stocks. "Warren Buffett believes that diversification is something people do to protect themselves from their own stupidity". (From Buffettology by Mary Buffett & David Clark). Mohnish Pabrai, hedge fund manager invests in 10 positions. Joel Greenblatt invests 80% of his millions in 5 ideas. When there is a tremendous opportunity invest a significant portion of your cash like 20 to 25% in one stock or even safer in a non-leveraged ETF like SPY, QQQ, DIA or IWM. ETF like QQQ is safer than an individual NASDAQ stock as it has 100 largest capitalized NASDAQ stocks.

You can buy and sell these using technical indicators. If you buy options on them, you can invest a small sum which is equal to buying a large number of QQQ shares. (You will read more about this later).

If you own ten stocks it would be good to invest in different industries so that when your sector goes down all your stocks would go down. Even so if you have an exit plan you can get out with minimal losses. Warren Buffett pays attention only to the company he is investing in. Only if it is a bargain he would buy. His teacher Benjamin Graham calls it "Margin of Safety". Also, the company has to fit his criteria of monopoly in their respective businesses; their products and services have wide, sustainable moats around them and very honest hard working and able management. He calculates the discounted future cash flow. He rarely sells. He keeps them for the compounding effect of the stock.

Some diversification is fine. Always buy the best, crème de la crème, the top company in the sector. Constantly keep looking for opportunities when the very best stocks are selling for cheap prices. As Charlie Munger put it "You are looking for mispriced gamble". This puts the odds greatly in your favor.

For example, Amazon (AMZN) stock has gone up from $61.69 (price adjusted for splits) on 3/6/2009, to $1861.69 as of 4/18/2019, a whopping appreciation of 2917.82%. If you used technical analysis, using a one-year one day chart, buying and selling Amazon stock, you would have made lot more money. For example, you could have sold the stock on 9/27/2018 for $2012.98 and you could have bought the same stock back on 12/24/2018 for $1343.96. From the profit you made on 9/27/2018 you could have bought more shares of AMZN. So, the best way to make lot of money is to trade more frequently based on one year and one day chart with technical analysis. (You will learn more later in this book).

Stock market is based on mass psychology. Sometimes there is panic and frenzy which leads to market crash. According to Bernard M. Baruch, had great investor of the past," These crowd madness recurs so frequently in human history". These crashes cause superb opportunities to pick up stocks on fire sale. Then the same market goes up irrationally and the stock prices go way over their intrinsic values. This situation of irrational exuberance creates opportunities to unload your stocks to those who are in a buying frenzy. Even without crashes, there are sectors and industry groups that are beaten down. This phenomenon happens due to sector rotation as mutual funds and other institutions sell their profitable stocks and invest in beaten down sectors. You can find gems in the beaten down stocks. But you may have to wait a year or even two for them to come up.

You will be delighted to see the results. Your stock could go up 50% or 100% or even higher.   Where do you find information on sectors? You can pick up a copy of Investors Business Daily or look it up in the library. Currently page 4 lists the top 40 industry groups and the worst 40 groups in the past six months. Even the best stocks get beaten down when the demand is below the supply. Usually most people are looking at the top groups but the value is in the bottom groups. *Markets will go higher than you think, and fall lower than you can possibly imagine,"* investing legend Jim Rogers said in the late 1980s book *Market Wizards.*

How do the Masters create huge profits in the stock market?
They pyramid their winnings stocks and sell their laggards early. If you want to make lot of money in the stock market, you have to change your habits.
If you bought ten stocks when the market hit a bottom and turned around, then keep following them closely. Then sell the number 10th ranked stock and buy stock ranked number one which is growing the fastest and so on. Watch them at the end of each day. Sell each stock when it goes down by 10% below the current price (mark to market), not 10% below the price you paid for. At some point before the market crashed you will be in cash with profits. Then wait patiently for the next opportunity.

What is the beauty of compounding?

Compounding is a very powerful tool. If you invest $10,000 at age 25 and it grows at 10% a year, compounded tax-free, will grow to $25,937 at age 35, $67,275 at age 45, $174,494 at age 55 and $452,593 at age 65. If it grows at 15% a year, at age 35 you will have $40,456, at age 45 $163,665, at age 55 $662,118 and at age 65 $ 2,678,635. If you invest $1200 every year from age 25 to age 65, at the rate of 10% a year compounded tax free, you will have $638,533. If it grows at 15% a year, you will have $2,776,581 when you retire at age 65. The importance is that the earlier you start, the more spectacular the results would be.

How do you gain the right knowledge?

Learn from the great books written by the wizards of Wall Street. "Without lifelong learning, you are not going to get very far in life based on what you already know". (Charlie Munger). Do not depend on newsletters.

Should you subscribe to newsletters?

No, if they give opinions only or theories. You can toss a coin instead.

Shoud you watch the business channels on TV?

Yes. Mute the volume. Do not listen to opinions and comments. They will make you confused; and then you will take the wrong action. Watch the ticker tape closely. Look for stocks that are crossing the tape frequently and going up. Positive price action in big volume, more than 100% of the average daily volume means that the institutional money is flowing into that particular stock. If they are already on your list, buy.

Look for opportunities; the very best stocks that are being beaten down severely; stocks that are going up in price, in strong volume. Follow the strongest leader in the ten strongest industry groups. Buy only if the market is in uptrend. The best time to buy is after a pull back when the market turns around.

What about the deflation and the stock market?

Securities decline during deflationary cycles. Cash is king during these periods. When the market bottoms and turns around there will be a great opportunity created. When this happens follow your list of best stocks. When the volume on any of these stocks goes way above the daily average volume, buy that.

What about inflation and the stock market?

During inflationary periods there is more money floating around which makes equities go up. Stocks are good as investment during inflationary cycles.

RECOMMENDED BOOKS FOR YOUR READING

*How I Made $2,000,000 In the Stock Market, By Nicolas Darvas

*The Battle for Investment Survival, by G. M. Loeb

*24 Essential Lessons for Investment Success by William J. O'Neil

*Mastering the Trade by John F. Carter

The Dhandho Investor by Pabrai

The Intelligent Investor Revised Edition by Benjamin Graham Updated by Jason Zweig

How to Make Money in Stocks by William J. O'Neil

The Successful Investor by William J. O'Neil

Real Money by James J. Cramer

Selling Cash Covered Puts by Alan Ellman

The Little Book That Still Beats the Market Updated by Greenblatt

Baruch My Own Story

The Book of Money by Agora Publishing Inc

Market Volatility Profit by Chuck Hughes and John Weston

RECOMMENDED FINANCIAL NEWSLETTERS THAT ARE BASED ON PROBABILITIES:

None.

I SUBSCRIBE TO THE FOLLOWING AND RECOMMEND HIGHLY:

Investors Business Daily online

Vectorvest

Markettrendsignal.com

I LOVE TO RECOMMEND THE FOLLOWING FREE ONLINE SERVICES:

Stockcharts.com

Finance.Yahoo.com

Nasdaq.com

https://optionseducation.org

PS: I do not have any financial interest in any of the business entities or companies mentioned in this book.

SELLING

LEARN TO SELL

Buying an equity is very easy. One click and you have bought. Selling is hard. When to sell is always the question. When an equity is going up, due to greed you may keep it forever and the eventually you may sell it for a loss. When you have 20% profits sell that much and transfer that amount to cash. If you do not do that the profits will disappear. So, you have to have an exit plan when you buy an equity and you have to write it down in a scrap book and you have to stick to that plan.

When you have a loss of about 10%, sell the whole equity. Every time you buy an equity (except for options which are very volatile) place a mental trailing stop order for 10% below the trading price. Do not place the trailing stop order with the broker. This way, you can take a ride with the stock as long as it goes up. Cut your losses early. You can sleep peacefully at night. When you stock keeps going up raise this mental trailing stop along with it. Do not wait until it falls below what you paid for.

Only when you sell you will have money to reinvest (when the market is down). If you are fully invested at all times, your account will go down when the market goes down. And you will not have cash to buy equities when they are on sale. You should not be in the market all the time. Hit and run is a good policy. You invest at the right time and exit at the right time.

Do not have any emotional attachment to any equity which may prevent you from selling at the right time. Being married to a stock is very bad and will end in disaster. You treat all the stocks as A, B, C or X, Y, Z. A good stock is one that goes up when you are invested in it.

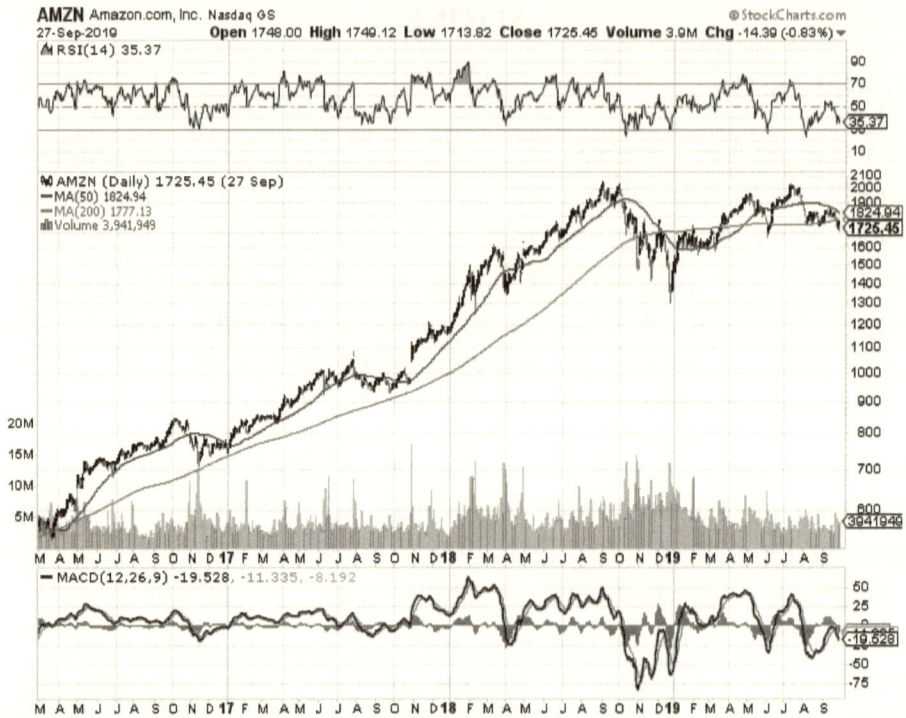

I use TD Ameritrade's Thinkorswim software which is free for the account holders. I use TTM Scalper Alert mainly. Also, I look at on balance volume, TTM Squeeze, RSI (length 4). TTM scalper alert generates buy and sell arrows. Whenever the trend changes you get a new signal. In any trend following methods there is some delay in the generation of these signals. Then you look at other parameters I mentioned. This has made me the most money.

You can use Stockcharts.com, which is free and use one year/daily chart and use the MACD to get in and out. When the black fast MACD line crosses from below the red slow MACD line you buy. When the reverse happens, you sell. Sometimes if the stock goes sideways it may not be very clear. Then you can use other technical indicators to help you make a decision; also look at your account which will tell you what is happening.

Buy and hold is not a strategy any more unless you are investing for your children's education or for retirement. There are people who tell you to buy and hold. I do not know why they tell others. All the institutional investors buy and sell. That is why the market goes up and down. Sometimes they own equities worth millions of dollars for only a few seconds. Please go to "Investopedia.com" and look up "Flash Trading".

Rich people have become richer because they know when to sell. They have learnt to sell. They buy only undervalued equities. They immediately determine their target price and get out at that price. Then they move their money into some other investment. You have to develop the courage to sell when everyone else is scrambling to buy. You see this phenomenon at the market tops. Have a note book and write down an exit plan for each equity at the time of purchase. Stick to your exit plan and follow it. Those who have the nerves of steel will surely win in this game.

Should you look for hundred percent appreciation?
No, except when you invest long term for children or for retirement. Even if you buy a stock that is trading at half its value, sell it when the technical indicators tell you so. You can always get back into that stock again later. Stocks will not go up in a straight line.

When and how should I take profits?
When your stocks are going up, keep taking profits. You may do that when your stocks go up by 20%. Otherwise the profits may disappear. Keep it in the form of cash. Of course, you can withdraw the money and use it. Keep rotating into stocks and back into cash. It should be like hit and run in baseball. Keep collecting runs. If your account grows from $10,000 to $15,000, if you do not take profits and suddenly the market tanks your $15,000 is vulnerable.

Can you donate your stock to a qualified charity?
Yes. You can donate your stock that has appreciated in value and take a deduction in taxes. You can use the market value on the date of donation by taking the average of the highest and the lowest trading price of that stock on that day.

TAXES

Every year you can deduct $3000 in capital losses. Anything over that limit you can carry forward indefinitely into future years. Please take note also of wash rule. I will give you an example. You bought XYZ shares for $20,000. Let us say, in November you sell all those shares for $15,000. You can show net capital losses of $3000. But if you buy back the same number of XYZ shares within 30 days of your selling, you cannot take any losses in that year. This is considered a wash sale.

If you sell any shares within one year of purchase, you have to pay short-term capital gain tax. This would be taxed at the same rate as your ordinary income.

If you sell any shares after holding for more than one year, then you pay long-term capital gain tax. You are taxed at a lower rate depending on your ordinary tax rate. This could vary from 0 to 20%.

If you owned shares for more than one year you can give those shares away as a charitable giving, and you can take a tax deduction for their current value. You may also consider giving those shares to your loved ones who are in lower tax brackets.

In the retirement accounts like IRAs and other pension plans you can defer paying taxes on any gains. This is true for short-term or long-term gains. But when you withdraw money from regular IRAs or pension plans, contributions and profits are taxed as ordinary income. Look into 529 College Savings Plan which allows individuals to save and invest on a tax-advantaged basis in order to fund future higher educational expenses for a child or other beneficiary. Look into Coverdell Education Savings Account. The money you invest grows tax deferred and proceeds can be withdrawn tax free for qualified education expenses at a qualified institution. It includes primary school to university.

Please consult your accountant to be sure as the tax laws keep changing all the time.

DOS AND DON'TS

Do not invest all your money in a single stock. I want to give you a couple of illustrations. On 2/24/2015 Biogen (BIIB) closed at $385. Earnings were announced before the market opened the next day. The stock opened at $326 and closed at $300. It went down by 22% in one day. Its market value went down by $20 billion in 24 hours! The company disclosed a sharp slowdown in sales growth of its multiple sclerosis drug and it slashed its earnings outlook for 2015.

The fundamentals of the company have been excellent as noted in Yahoo Finance on 7/25/2014. Its cash flow was $1.38 billion for the period ending December 31, 2012 and it had gone up to $2.93 billion by December 31, 2014. Looking at the balance sheet of December 31, 2014, the total current assets were $4.67 billion and total assets of $14.3 billion. The total liabilities were only $3.5 billion. This company has been rich in cash and they have more than enough current assets to pay off all their liabilities any time. Their operating margin was 45%, return of equity of 31% and quarterly earnings growth of 30%. The revenue growth was only fair at 7%.

What do we learn from this? On the day of earnings announcement, even a stock with excellent fundamentals can crash. If you happen to have a lot of money invested in a single stock, a day or two before the earnings announcement (you can find the date in Yahoo Finance), you can sell the stock or buy a put option at the money for protection. Your risk depends on how many stocks are in your portfolio. If you own 10 stocks the risk is 10% per stock. You may consider investing in an ETF like QQQ. The risk of investing in QQQ is 1% per stock as QQQ has 100 largest companies NASDAQ, called NASDAQ 100.

A stock can suddenly drop, even if it is not the earnings announcement date. On 5/2/2012 Green Mountain Coffee, GMCR closed at $50. The next day it closed at $26. It had excellent fundamentals and the drop was due to some rumor. Professionals short stocks and then create rumors to bring the stock prices down.

Place a 10% mental trailing stop loss as soon as you buy a stock. This will protect your assets. You do not have to watch your stocks constantly and you can sleep peacefully. Some stocks can keep going up for months raking up huge profits.

Never sell a naked call option as the losses can be unlimited.

While watching business channel on television mute it. If you listen you may register lot of unwanted information in your subconscious mind which will lead you to making wrong decisions at the important moments. There is too much information out there and most of it is noise. The noise is created by people for their own benefit and not yours.

Never subscribe to financial newsletters that give you probabilities. You can flip a coin on your own.

Never buy and hold any equity.

Never listen to analysts.

Never listen to Wall Street rumors.

Do not get scared when the market crashes. You should have been out of the market way before that. If you had placed a mental trailing stop on each stock purchase, you should be in cash by this time. When the market crashes it creates a 'sale' in the equities and you can buy them when the trend changes to uptrend. Look for stocks with sudden increase in price and volume. This means that institutions are buying. About 85% of money in Wall Street belongs to institutions. Only 15% belongs to individuals like you and me. We do not have control of the market. We cannot change the market but the institutions can and they do.

Adopt a cool unemotional attitude like Clint Eastwood in Pale Rider.

Never listen to anyone in a party about stocks and this will affect your plans and will affect your courage to pull the trigger at the right moment.

Have a scrap book and write down when you have a loss and the reason for it, so that you do not repeat it.

Never have a broker call you. Never take his advice. His company may be pushing a stock on their clients.

Pay attention to rising industry groups and sectors. Remember that changes occur at the beginning a quarter and at the beginning of a new cycle after a bear market.

Read Wiiliam O'Neil's book on How to Make Money in Stocks and learn about recognizing chart patterns like cup and handle, saucer and handle, etc. You can pick up stocks when they break out. Learn his 'CANSLIM' method to pick great stocks. In the Investors Daily I write down the stock symbols of stocks in the 95th to the 99th percentile ranking based on their earnings per share on the first of each month. My list changes every month.

You should also learn candle stick patterns. This was invented by Munehisa Homma in Japan in the 1700s. From these patterns which change according to the opening price, closing price, up or down of any equity, you can predict the future movement of the equity. You can use in the minute chart to weekly or even monthly chart successfully if you recognize the patterns. You can learn them in Wikipedia.com or Stockcharts.com and click on ChartSchool.

INVESTING FOR CHILDREN'S EDUCATION

Education costs are very high and they keep going up all the time. You will be extremely happy if you plan and invest for children many years before they go to college. Due to the beauty of compounding you will be amazed by the numbers achieved when your children join college, even if you invest what looks like a small amount. Later on, when you withdraw money and pay for college expenses, you do not pay any taxes. This is a significant advantage. The earlier you start investing the better the results will be.

Coverdell ESA (Education Savings Account): As soon as your child is born you can get a social security number and open an ESA account in a brokerage company which is financially strong. Your contributions are limited to $2000 dollars a year. You can contribute yearly until the child is 18. The growth of the investment is not taxed. Distributions are not taxed when used for educational purposes. Distributions have to be made before the age of 30. If any money is not used for educational expenses, then the balance is taxed to the beneficiary.

Please read the rules and regulations in detail from the IRS site: https://www.irs.gov/taxtopics/tc310. You can invest the money for your child. Let us say you invest $2000 a year from birth to age 18 in QQQ. QQQ has gone up by 18% annually in the last 10 years as of 2/29/2020 (information from Invesco.com website). At age of 18 your child's account will have $284,174! (I used the compound interest calculator found at www.moneychimp.com. I added the $2000 in the beginning of each year). You can check this out at this website.

529 Plan: A 529 plan is a tax-advantaged savings plan designed to encourage savings for future education costs. There are two types of plans: Prepaid Tuition Plans and Education Savings Plans. These accounts are offered by different brokerage firms. You should carefully review the offering circular of each plan and discuss with the broker in detail. There are fees associated with these plans. Many different plans are available and hey invest in mutual funds, exchange traded funds or principal protected bank product. You can choose whatever product you like. I like to recommend investing in large cap ETF funds. In the long run they will give you the best returns. You have to compare the results of such program in different brokerage firms and choose the best one.

Many states offer tax benefits for contributions to a 529 plan. Growth in these accounts are not subject to federal income tax and in many cases state income tax. If the 529 plan withdrawals are not used for qualified higher education expenses or tuition for elementary or secondary schools, they will be subject to state and federal income taxes and an additional 10% tax penalty on the earnings.

Please visit the following site and read thoroughly the rules and regulations: **https://www.sec.gov**

INVESTING IN INDEX EXCHANGE TRADED FUNDS (ETFs)

This is my favorite investment. It is more conservative and less risky when compared to investing in individual stocks. Warren Buffett feels that non-professionals should stick to index funds. There are four large index ETFs you should look at. They are SPY, QQQ, DIA, and IWM. You can buy and sell these in your brokerage account like stocks. Index funds have low expense ratios.

SPY is S&P 500 SPDR ETF. It invests in the 500 common stocks in the S&P 500 Index. SPY represents investment in a blend of large capitalization stocks representing many industry groups from aerospace and defense to utilities. The weight of each stock in the portfolio is similar to that in the index. For example, more money will be invested in Apple Inc (market cap of $998 billion on 5/3/2019) when compared to Berkshire Hathaway B shares (market capitalization of $358 million on 5/3/2019). As of 5/3/2019 S&P gave a yield of 1.39%. The average daily volume traded was 55,502,453 as of 2/11/2015.

QQQ is Powershares QQQ Trust ETF. It seeks daily investment results that correspond to the daily performance of NASDAQ-100 Index which represents the largest non-financial domestic and international stocks (and no energy or utility stocks). This index is heavy in technology stocks. QQQ is market capitalization weighted like SPY. On 5/3/2019 more money would have been invested in Apple, Google and Microsoft due to the weighting. As of 5/3/2019 the 12-month dividend yield was 0.52%. On 5/3/2019 the volume traded was 30,307,864.

DIA is SPDR Dow Jones Industrial Average ETF. DIA corresponds to the price and yield performance of the Dow Jones Industrial Average (DJIA). It holds a portfolio of stocks that are included in the DJIA. This is also market capitalization weighted. As of 5/3/2019 dividend the yield was 2.29%. the volume traded was 2,158,154.

IWM is i Shares Russell 2000 ETF. It tracks the investment results of small-capitalization U.S. equities. As of 5/3/2019 the dividend yield was 1.16%. The volume reported on the same day was 19,930,371.

The following is my recommendation using Stockcharts.com. This is a wonderful free website. Enter QQQ in the box on top to the right of "Create a Chart" and "Sharp Chart". You will get a chart for 6 months. It has RSI (Relative Strength Index), candlestick chart, volume and MACD (Moving Average Convergence Divergence). Below all these you can find Chart Attributes, Overlays, Indicators, Gallery View, Point & Figure Chart Perf chart and Seasonality Chart. I do not stay invested in any of the indices all the time. I use a hit and run method like in baseball. You use the MACD graph. When the fast-moving line (in black at this time) moves above the slow-moving line (in red at this time) you invest your money. You will also see the MACD as a bar chart also where the line chart of MACD is. When the MACD fast moving line crosses from above to below the slow-moving line, you sell the QQQ and go to cash and wait for the next opportunity. Every few weeks you have to act. You may also learn how to use the other parameters by clicking on CHARTSCHOOL on top. Pay attention to the general market direction. If the market is in correction, you cannot make money going long.

WHY DO I LIKE QQQ?

SINCE 3-24-2009 TO 3-28-2019

QQQ HAS GONE UP BY 488%

IWM HAS GONE UP BY 267%

SPY HAS GONE UP BY 248%

DIA HAS GONE UP BY 235%

Personally, I like to use QQQ out of these four. QQQ has 100 underlying large capitalization stocks and you are all 100 stocks together and you do not have the risk of investing and depending on one individual stock. The risk is lower here. When the market is trending down you are out of the market. There is no method which will put you in at the exact bottom and take you out at the exact top. But you will be close. When the market is choppy you may be in and out frequently but in general only once in a few weeks you have to buy or sell. By following hit and run method you will make much more than the numbers given above.

Again, the general market direction is very important. You invest in QQQ when the market is in uptrend. How do you find the trend? You can go to the library and look at the "Big Picture" in Investors Business Daily. Or you can look at the graphs of Dow Jones Industrial Average, S&P 500 Index and NASDAQ index in Stockcharts.com. Or you can subscribe to Vectorvest.com and Markettrendsignal.com.

Also look at the seasonality chart for QQQ in Stockcharts.com.

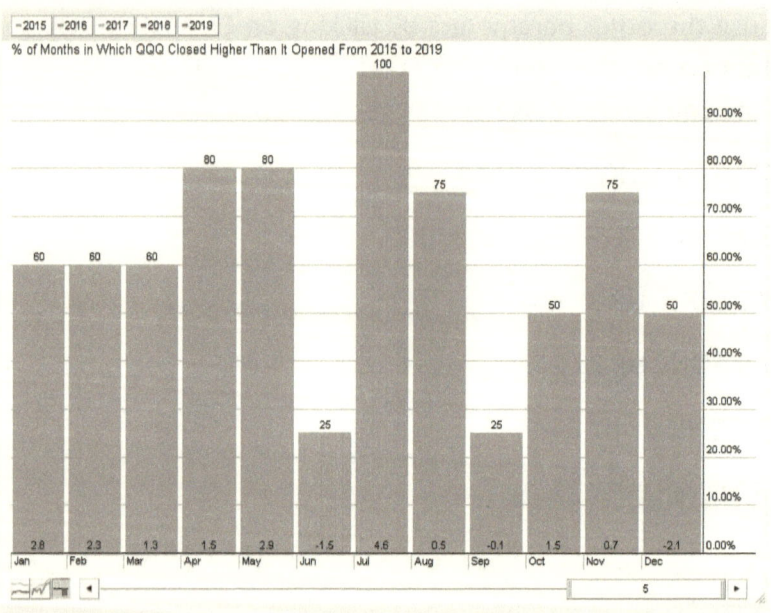

"Chart courtesy of stockcharts.com"

Summary:

- I like investing in ETFs rather than in stocks, like SPY, DIA, IWM and QQQ.
- I love QQQ because it has outperformed the others for the past several years.
- QQQ tracks NASDAQ 100 index which has 100 large cap stocks like MSFT, GOOGL, AAPL and FB.
- Use technical indicators to trade these.

MY VERY BEST STRATEGY AND MY VERY BEST RECOMMENDATION FOR YOUR RETIREMENT AND FOR CHILDREN'S EDUCATION (INVESTING NOT TRADING)

This method is slow and boring and if you give 10 years are more it will make mind boggling amount of money. It is base on the beauty of compounding. You buy an ETF called QQQ every two weeks. You invest the fixed amount of dollars and buy as many QQQ is possible for that amount. The market will go up, down or sideways. You close your eyes and stick to your plan. When you retire or when your child goes to college you will be amazed when you look at your accounts. It is not possible to make by trading stocks by yourself to equal the annual appreciation of QQQ. You have to be strong willed and stick to the plan.

Let us say that you start investing $ 6,000 a year starting at age 30 in IRA. You add $6,000 a year at the beginning of each year. (Or you can invest $500 a month and your final figure will be even bigger than investing once a year). Because of the ease of calculating I have used examples of investing once a year in the beginning of the year. The results will be different if you calculate using investment done once a year at the end of the year.

All you do is keep on buying only QQQ in your retirement account at the current price of QQQ. The growth rate in the past 15 years of QQQ has been 29%. I used the compound interest calculator found in www.moneychimp.com. Let us say, you start investing at age 30 and retire at 65. You invest $6000 a year in the beginning of the year in QQQ. Here are the findings: At 65 you will have $242,662,371. This is unbelievable but true. You can calculate it for yourself. You can ask your accountant to verify this. This is very similar to how cancer cells divide, double and grow to billions!

There are two main reasons for this phenomenal growth. One is due to the long period of 35 years, with growth on growth added every year. The other factor is the high growth rate of 29%. This growth rate is from 9/27/2004 to 9/27/2019 (fifteen years). This period includes the significant drop in the stock market in the 2008/2009 period.

The inception date of QQQ was 3/10/1999. I could calculate only from 4/23/1999 to 9/27/2019. On 4/23/1999 it was trading at $55.32. On 9/27/2019 it was trading at $187.03. During that period, it had gone up by 238.12% or at an annualized rate of 11.65%. This period includes the dotcom bust in year 2000. Even if you use the annualized growth rate of 11.65% and invest $6000 a year for 35 years you will still have $2,947,494. You will still be a millionaire. Of course, QQQ has been doing much better in the past 15 years in spite of the huge market correction in 2008-2009. This is because of the growth seen in companies like Microsoft, Apple, Amazon, Facebook, Google, etc. In year 2000 the drop in the market was due to irrational exuberance when people invested huge amounts of money in small worthless companies which led to the dotcom bubble and bust. If you study the list of companies in QQQ you will be impressed by the quality and strength of the underlying companies. These are not tiny companies. For example, Microsoft and Apple have market caps currently of over $1 trillion!

A friend of mine started investing in mutual funds in his IRA account around age 30. Every month he was adding to his portfolio. At 65 he had a few million dollars.

The reasons for his success are: choosing the best funds, discipline in adding to the portfolio once a month irrespective of the net asset value of these funds and the snowballing effect of growth over 35 years.

Better than this story is about another doctor friend of mine who started investing in S&P 500 index at age 35. He was adding money every month irrespective of the price of S&P 500 index.

At 65 he retired with several million dollars. He chose S&P 500 index over mutual funds is because the cost of owning index funds is much lower than the expense ratio of mutual funds and the ease of investing in index funds. Also, most mutual funds do not beat S&P 500 index.

Better than investing in S&P 500 index is investing in QQQ. In the past 15 years QQQ has beaten S&P 500 hands down. It has beaten DIA (which tracks Dow Jones Industrial Average) and IWM which tracks Russell 2000 small cap index). It has even beaten Warren Buffett's Berkshire Hathaway A shares. Please see the table below.

SYMBOL	START DATE	START PRICE	END DATE	END PRICE	% PRICE CHANGE	% ANNUALIZED RATE OF RETURN
	9/27/2004		9/27/2019			
QQQ		34.5		187.03	442.12	29.46
BRKA		86.2		311.45	261.31	17.41
VTI		53.38		150.3	181.57	12.1
IWM		55.74		151.16	171.21	11.41
DIA		100.16		267.99	167.56	11.16
SPY		110.75		295.4	166.73	11.11

QQQ is Invesco QQQ Trust
SPY is SPDR S&P 500 ETF
BRKA is Berkshire Hathaway A shares (in thousands of dollars)
VTI is Vanguard Total Stock Market Index ETF
IWM is iShares Russell 2000 Index ETF
DIA is SPDR Dow Jones Industrial Average ETF

QQQ Invesco QQQ Trust

For data click this link
(https://www.invesco.com/usrest/contentdetail?contentId=3a48e01e9
8630410 VgnVCM10000046f1bf0aRCRD&dnsName=us)

The above is a weekly chart of QQQ courtesy of Stockcharts.com (charts, tools and education are available free and with subscription). Even though stock market has dips on and off look at the growth of the price at a 45* angle! It is very impressive.

Even if the market goes down for a few months or even a few years, the market always will come back and make new highs. Bear markets do not last forever and at some point, the market turns around and goes up. When the market is going down you are sticking to the plan of buying QQQ, let us say monthly. Then you are dollar cost averaging. You end result will be much better than investing a lump sum once a year. You will be getting better prices of QQQ when the market goes down.

Listen to what the greatest investor of all time says. These quotations are like gems:

"If you invested in a very low-cost index fund -- where you don't put the money in at one time, but average in over 10 years -- you'll do better than 90% of people who start investing at the same time". Warren Buffett

"A good investor always plays the long game. Moving around is not smart in investing. Many investors make the mistake of constantly buying and selling stocks, rather than holding onto their investments to give them time to mature and potentially make more money over time". Warren Buffett

Buffett says, "If you hold on to a diverse selection of stocks for long enough, then the market should eventually trend upward. I know what markets are going to do over a long period of time: They're going to go up. But in terms of what's going to happen in a day or a week or a month or a year even, I've never felt that I knew it and I've never felt that was important,"

Let me ask you a question. Have you made 29% per year in the past 15 years by investing on your own, especially by buying and selling stocks? If not please consider following this method to victory.

Starting to invest earlier than later makes a huge difference in the final outcome. Let us go to our example of investing $6000 a year in tax deferred plan at the beginning of the year, for 35 years (from age 30 to 65) at a growth rate of 29% a year, you will have at age 65 $ 242,662,371! I used the compound interest calculator at www.moneychimp.com.

Instead if you start at age of 35 and invest for 30 years (from age 35 to 65) at a growth rate of 29% a year, you will have at age 65, $ 67,909,573. Still you have over $67 million.

In the above method, I have used only an investment of $6,000 per year. Of course, you can invest more for your retirement. Please consult your account, who will create the right retirement plan for you. Imagine if you can put away $30,000 a year from age 30 to 65, at the start of the year, and it grows at 29% per year, you will have $ 1,213,311,853! over one billion dollars!! This astronomical number is real. You please check it out. Even if you started at age 35 the end result will be $ 339,547,863, over $339 million! Let your accountant verify these figures. For above calculations, I did the additions at the start of the year.

You may have a question, what if QQQ grows only at 19% a year? If you invest $30,000 a year from age 30 to 65 you will end up with a sum of $95,838,448, not bad! What if the growth rate of QQQ is only 11.65% a year, you still will have $14,737,468, not shabby! (The launch date of QQQ was on 4/23/1999. Until 9/27/2019 it had grown on an average annual rate of 11.65%).

What happens if you invest monthly instead of annually? The results are even better. These were calculated using Microsoft Excel. If you invest annually $6000 at the end of the year for 35 years at a growth rate of 29%, you will have $153,579,981! (over $153 million). If you invest $500 a month for 420 months (35 years), at a growth rate of 2.42% a month (29% a year), you will have $475,050,500!! (over $475 million). What happens if you invest on the 1st and 15th of each month?

Let me ask you a question. Have you made 29% per year in the past 15 years by investing on your own, especially by buying and selling stocks? If not please consider following this method to victory.

Starting to invest earlier than later makes a huge difference in the final outcome. Let us go to our example of investing $6000 a year in tax deferred plan at the beginning of the year, for 35 years (from age 30 to 65) at a growth rate of 29% a year, you will have at age 65 $ 242,662,371! I used the compound interest calculator at www.moneychimp.com.

Instead if you start at age of 35 and invest for 30 years (from age 35 to 65) at a growth rate of 29% a year, you will have at age 65, $ 67,909,573. Still you have over $67 million.

In the above method, I have used only an investment of $6,000 per year. Of course, you can invest more for your retirement. Please consult your account, who will create the right retirement plan for you. Imagine if you can put away $30,000 a year from age 30 to 65, at the start of the year, and it grows at 29% per year, you will have $ 1,213,311,853! over one billion dollars!! This astronomical number is real. You please check it out. Even if you started at age 35 the end result will be $ 339,547,863, over $339 million! Let your accountant verify these figures.   For above calculations, I did the additions at the start of the year.

You may have a question, what if QQQ grows only at 19% a year? If you invest $30,000 a year from age 30 to 65 you will end up with a sum of $95,838,448, not bad! What if the growth rate of QQQ is only 11.65% a year, you still will have $14,737,468, not shabby! (The launch date of QQQ was on 4/23/1999. Until 9/27/2019 it had grown on an average annual rate of 11.65%).

What happens if you invest monthly instead of annually? The results are even better. These were calculated using Microsoft Excel. If you invest annually $6000 at the end of the year for 35 years at a growth rate of 29%, you will have $153,579,981! (over $153 million). If you invest $500 a month for 420 months (35 years), at a growth rate of 2.42% a month (29% a year), you will have $475,050,500!! (over $475 million). What happens if you invest on the 1st and 15th of each month?

If you invest $250 each time, at a growth rate of 1.21% (29% a year) 840 times (35 years), you will end up with $504,444,895!! (super-duper). This illustrates the fact that investing twice a month is even better. Several leading brokerage firms allow you to buy even one share of QQQ without paying any commission. Isn't it great?

Let me calculate using Microsoft Excel for compounding. If you invest $30,000 annually at the end of the year for 35 years you will have $767,899,907 at a growth rate of 29% a year. Instead if you invest $2500 a month over 420 periods (35 years), at a growth rate of 2.42% a month (29% a year), the results are amazing.........$2,375,252,500! If you invest $1250 twice a month ($30,000 a year) at a growth rate of 1.21% (29% a year), you will have a several million more dollars!! ($2,522,224,477).

As you know, at this time, many leading brokerage firms let you buy ETFs without any commission. Every penny you invest goes to work for your retirement!!

Please have faith; close your eyes; keep following the method; be firm in your commitment; you will surely succeed.

My accountant/CPA has read this book and liked it a lot. He is a professor of accounting in a university. He asked me to address his young students who loved the data. He is very knowledgeable in the stock market and has been trading stocks, options and futures successfully. He loved my simple and a great method. He is young and has started buying QQQ every two weeks. I feel flattered and happy that my CPA has applied this method for himself! It is like attestation!!

SUMMARY

- Even when the market goes down you will be adding to your positions and getting better prices.
- Read the quotations from the great master, Warren Buffett on long term investing.
- Investing $6000 a year from age 30 to 65 at a growth rate of 29% a year will give you a retirement nest egg of $242,662,371 (Compound interest calculator... www.moneychimp.com).

- If you put away $30,000 a year from age 30 to 65 at a growth rate of 29% a year, you will have $1,213,311,828! (over one billion dollars. It is real. Please calculate for yourself and start believing in this method).
- Starting to invest earlier than later makes a huge difference in the final outcome.
- The best way is to invest a fixed amount of money by buying QQQ at the ask price, on the 1st and the 15th of each month in your brokerage account where you pay no commissions. You will have humongous amount of money when you retire. Always invest in the financially sound brokerage firms and make sure that your account is SIPC insured. You look at how much each account is insured for. Eventually you may need several accounts so that each one of your accounts is insured.
- Take this book seriously. Study the book. Show it to your accountant. Then on your mark, get set, go…………to victory!

SELLING CASH COVERED PUTS

This is a favorite investment of mine.

You can sell naked puts but you have to have a margin account with adequate cash in the account to cover. Naked means that you are selling a put option without owning the underlying security. So, if the put option is exercised the underlying equity will be assigned to your account. I like to sell puts on index ETFs like QQQ, SPY, IWM or DIA and not on individual stocks, as the risk is higher with individual stocks. I also like to use the weekly options. Time decay (theta) is your best friend in this formula and closer to the expiration date, the time decay is faster.

I will give you an example. I am writing this on 2/14/15 which is a Saturday. QQQ closed at 106.91 on 2/13/15. I go to Finance.Yahoo.com and scroll through the put options listed which will expire on 2/20/15. The put option closest to the closing price of 106.91 is 106.50. So, I choose this. One option covers 100 shares of QQQ. Let us say that I sell 10 contracts of the February 20th 2015 $106.50 put option. In the account I should have $106,500. The closing bid price on February 13, 2015 was $0.52. On Monday 2/16/15 the premium may be slightly different. If QQQ closes on Friday February 20th at any price higher than 106.50, I keep $520 minus the commission. If it closes below that price, on Monday 2/23/15 I will find 100 shares of QQQ in my account. Of course, I keep the $520 minus the commission.

The advantage of selling a put option is that, money comes into the account first. That is why, this strategy is a favorite of the rich. If you have a good gain in the next couple of days after you sell the put, you can close the option by buying it back at a lower price. Sell a put option only if QQQ is in an uptrend.

How do I determine the trend for QQQ? I use Stockcharts.com. This is a wonderful free website. Enter QQQ in the box on top to the right of "Create a Chart" and "Sharp Chart". You will get a chart for 6 months. It has RSI (Relative Strength Index), candlestick chart, volume and MACD (Moving Average Convergence Divergence). Below all these you can find Chart Attributes, Overlays, Indicators, Gallery View, Point & Figure Chart Perf chart and Seasonality Chart. Look at the seasonality chart for QQQ. This will show you the best times to make money using QQQ.

I use a hit and run method like in baseball. I use the MACD graph. When the fast-moving line (in black at this time) moves above the slow-moving line (in red at this time) I sell the put option expiring next Friday. When the MACD fast moving line crosses from above to below the slow-moving line, I stop using the above strategy and wait for the next opportunity.

There a leveraged ETF. These have higher volatility. You can make more money with these or lose more money as they are leveraged. To study you can go to Direxioninvstments.com. There are other ones also. You can look up the following symbols: TNA, TZA, TQQQ, SQQQ, SPXL, UPRO, SPXU, UDOW and SDOW. I use TNA and TQQQ almost all the time. I sell cash covered weekly puts if these are in uptrend. I stay in cash otherwise.

If you have a favorite stock, you can do the same. If the stock goes down, the stock will be assigned to you and strike price you sold the put for. As you like the stock, you do not mind having it in the account.

INVESTING IN VIX, VXX AND VIXY

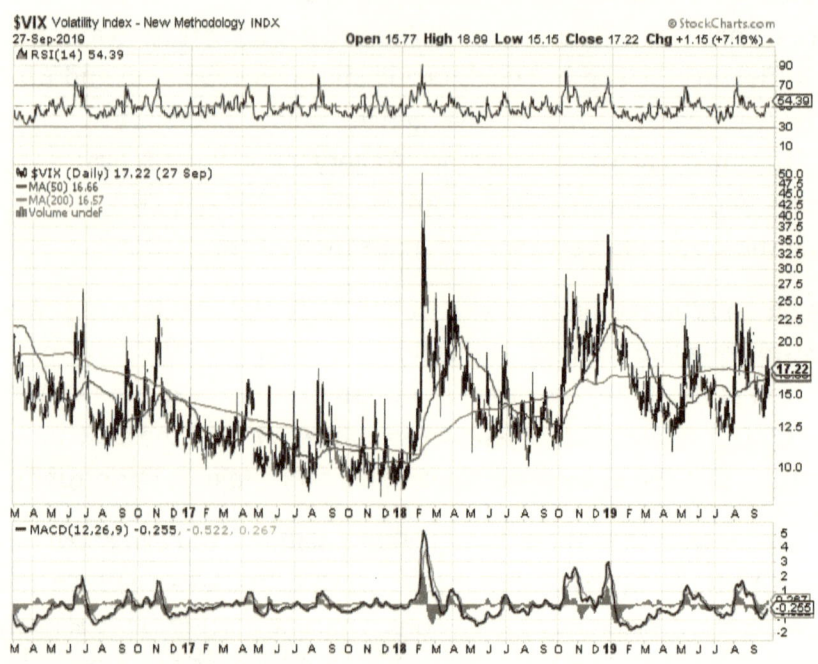

"Chart courtesy of stockcharts.com"

First of all, I want to define VIX. VIX is the ticker symbol for the Chicago Board of Options Exchange (CBOE) volatility index. It is a measure of the implied volatility of S&P 500 index options over the next 30 days. It is also called the fear index. It is a measure of perceived volatility. When the market is expected to drop, the VIX goes up and vice versa. You can buy call and put options on VIX.

Also look at VXX and VIXY.

VXX is an ETN (Exchange-traded Note), which you can buy and sell during market hours like a stock. It is iPath S&P 500 VIX Short-Term Futures ETN. You can buy VXX or options. It moves in parallel to VIX.

VIXY is an Exchange Traded Fund. It is run by ProShares. It represents VIX Short-Term Futures. It moves in parallel to VIX.

From August 6th 2015 to September 6th VXX and VIXY went up over 80%. Remember that these are good for short term trading only and you have to study them and understand the risks if you want to trade them. You can also trade options on these and thus invest smaller amounts of money.

MAGICFORMULAINVESTING.COM

This Is a free website.

This method of investing has been explained in a beautiful small book written by Mr. Joel Greenblatt called "The Little Book that still beats the market". Mr. Greenblatt explains that you can find stocks that are worth $1000, selling for $500. This is because Mr. Market, as called by Mr. Benjamin Graham, can have wild mood swings. When you buy shares at a discount to true value, you are getting the margin of safety. When you are buying at bargain prices, the price/earnings ratio would be low and so the earnings yield (which is 100 divided by P/E ratio) would be high. The second important factor is that you are investing in stocks of companies which yield a high return of capital.

MAGICFORMULAINVESTING.COM gives you a stock screener. You can choose stocks with a minimum market capitalization of $50 million to $5 billion. You can choose 30 to 50 stocks. Then click on "Get stocks". You will get a list of stocks. These stocks are currently selling at bargain prices based on their low price/earnings ratios (based on last year's earnings) and high return of capital. Buy a portfolio of 30 stocks. If you have profits you hold them for one year and one day. Sell the stocks that you have losses in, just before the end of one year. Then invest in a new portfolio. This way you will pay less capital gains tax. From 1988 to 2004 owning a portfolio of 30 stocks has appreciated by 30.8% per year. During the same period S&P 500 grew by 12.4%.

This is phenomenal. During the first year of investment you can buy 2 or 3 stocks a month. This way you will average into the market. When you are starting, if the market has gone down and you are just starting, you may buy all 30 stocks at the market bottom. You can find the market bottom by following Investor Business Daily, in The Big Picture section, under market outlook or by subscribing to Vectorvest.com. Buying a lower number of stocks will be riskier. You can choose large capitalization stocks or small capitalization stocks or a mix depending on your liking. In general, large cap stocks are safer but the small cap stocks grow faster. Between 1988 and 2009 a portfolio investing in the largest 1000 stocks with over $1 billion in market capitalization yielded growth of 19.7% versus 23.8% for a portfolio investing in the largest 3500 stocks with market capitalization of over $50 million. These yields include the negative years like 2002, 2007 and 2008.

I recommend that you buy this book called "The Little Book that still beats the market" and read it.

INVESTING IN OPEN-ENDED MUTUAL FUNDS

As of November 2014, there were approximately 8000 open-ended mutual funds in the United States and over $15 billion were invested in these funds. In the past few years part of the money has been going out of these funds into exchange traded funds called ETFs. On an average about 50% of these funds beats S&P 500 index in the span of one to five years. If you look at a period of 20 years only 15% of these funds beats S&P 500 index. These funds charge a fee called expense ratio. This is true for even the so-called no-load funds. There are load funds which may charge a front-end load, which you pay when you get in. Some funds charge rear end and load when you get out. When these funds have capital gains or dividends, they pass them on to the shareholders. These are taxable to the shareholders unless you are investing IRA or pension money. You can buy these funds directly from the investment companies or through your stockbroker. If your order a sell during the day you will get the NAV (net asset value) after the close of the market.

If you want to invest in open-ended mutual funds, I recommend buying a copy of Investors Business Daily or looking it up in the library. They list the top growth fund in the last 3 months and in the last 36 months. I prefer the 3 months list. Choose only from A+ rated ones.

INVESTING IN IPOs

IPOs are initial public offerings. Private companies go public by this means. This process is done by underwriting firms. The company shares are allotted to institutional investors, preferred individual clients and high net worth individuals who have large accounts in these firms and in major brokerage houses.

The rewards of investing in IPOs can be breath taking based on the study by Ibbotson, Sindelar and Ritter (1994). Starting in January 1960 if one had invested $1000 in a random sample of IPOs and selling after one month and then buying a new set of IPOs in the next month and repeating the same until December of 2001 the investment would have grown to $533 multiplied by 1 followed by 33 zeros!. During the same period if one had invested equal amount of money in a value-weighted portfolio it would have grown to $74,000.

IPOs are very popular at the time of this publication. For example, stock of Gopro Inc Cl A was offered on 6/24/2014 by J P Morgan at $24. It went public on 7/9/2014. It opened at $43.01. On 10/9/2014 it closed at $89.18, up by 271.6% in 3 months.

Ordinary folks have no chance of buying an IPO before it goes public. So, what do we do? We can invest in First Trust US IPO ETF (symbol: FPX). This was the first ETF created that invests in IPOs. ETFs are exchange traded funds which can be bought and sold like stocks. ETFs boast low management fees. FPX has an annual fee of 0.60%. Its most recent annual yield was 0.77%. FPX is a non-diversified, modified value-weighted price index investing in top ranked U S Companies by capitalization. The index is updated quarterly. I feel that the risk is lower with large capitalization companies than small ones.

This ETF came public on May 24, 2006 at $18.77 and on 2/6/15 it closed at 50.44.
You can go to "http://finance.yahoo.com" and "www.Investopedia.com" and look it up. Some of the rules it follows are given below: It excludes stocks with market capitalization lower than $50 million. To avoid possible initial hype, it waits for seven days after the stock goes public before it buys. On the 1000th day of trading it sells that stock. The following is my opinion. I like FPX as a simple tool for investing in IPOs.
http://schwert.ssb.rochester.edu/hbfech15.pdf

INVESTING IN INDEXED UNIVERSAL LIFE INSURANCE

What are the benefits of such an investment? First of all, that is no risk to the principal. There is no limit to your contribution. An employer of a corporation can have his or her own investment and there is no penalty to exclude employees. Your contribution will be made with after-tax money. But the growth of the invested money is not taxed. Also, there is tax-free retirement income and tax-free death benefit.

Please understand that there are fees, mortality charges, expense charges and surrender charges. You should consult your accountant regarding taxes and may get legal advice applicable to your circumstances. Various life insurance companies offer this program and you should compare. You may invest a lump sum. Or you may choose to invest every year for five years and then stop contributing. Usually this policy carries an annual interest which is credited to your account. Also, the policy is indexed to S & P 500 index. You may find policies indexed to Russell 2000, bonds, etc. The growth of S&P 500 is added as an interest credit to your account and this is capped. If the S&P 500 has a negative year, that interest credit to your account would be 0% and not minus. If you surrender the policy prematurely that would be fees and taxes owed. Overall this is an excellent way of investing and also having the benefits of the life insurance.

FOLIOINVESTING.COM

I recommend you to look at a website called "FOLIOINVESTING.COM". You can trade as much as you need, in as many accounts as you want, and with as many portfolios as you like, all for a flat rate of $29 per month (with some restrictions). You can customize their ready-made portfolios, build your own or follow an expert. They have over 160 pre-made portfolios to choose from. This company was started by Mr. Steven M.H. Wallman who was a commissioner with Securities and Exchange Commission.

AMAZING NEW CHANGES

I am writing this in June of 2020. In 1970s have paid even 1.2% in brokerage commission one way. Then you have to make 2.4% even to break even. Amazing changes have happened. We have to thank Charles Schwab for initiating the wave of price cuts. In October of 2019 Charles Schwab slashed their fees from $4.95 to 0. Others followed suit shortly. Imagine the tremendous advantage to us, customers. We can buy and sell even one share or thousands of shares without paying a penny and as frequently as we want.

Another great boon for investors is the possibility of buying fraction of a share. In November of 2019 Interactive Brokers became the first one to offer this feature. In January 2020 Fidelity announced the same. What is the greatness of this feature? Suppose you want to save $500 a month and you want to invest in QQQ, yes you can. All $500 will be invested in QQQ and even if QQQ is trading at $235 you will own 2.127 shares. You can keep investing $500 a month and every penny will be invested in QQQ regardless of what it is trading at. This method is called dollar cost averaging as you know. You can invest $100 in each of stocks like Amazon, Apple, Google, etc. This is unbelievable! You can connect your brokerage account to your bank and you can transact using a cell phone! This is a superb method if you want to investment for your retirement. It is the best method to becoming a millionaire!

www.ingramcontent.com/pod-product-compliance
Lightning Source LLC
Chambersburg PA
CBHW020614220526
45463CB00006B/2587